The Mystery of Love

Daisy Mai Hilton 2024 ©

"The mystery of love is greater than the mystery of death"

-Oscar Wilde, 1891

Dear reader,
    I hope my cliches for romanticism are understandable, I hope my artwork feeds in to those cliches and effects the way I write, I hope that if you can relate to my words that you are healing or are healed, I hope my work can help you recognize the healthy and unhealthy sides to a relationship, so you can be safe, happy and loved.

Contents

The beauty of love and self-love.

-My sweet baby, my sweet boy

-Art created on the rose

-Sweet as sugar

-The eyes

-To experience love is as lucky as to experience happiness

-Whispers in the night

-Fairies

-Empress or the other woman?

-I am enough

- Definition

- Sea

- As I spread my wings angelic, I shine
- Affirmations

- Not his show girl

The poisonous venom from love.

-Scribble, scribble out my heart

-Your dream girl?

-An angel's ego

-Snooker bar

-Show girl

-Cocaine heart

-Craving for love not lust

-Falling away

-Loneliness

-HD & replay

-Caution flammable

-Fragile masculinity

-Be free, be free, be free

-A cruel dance of violence

-I wished for our forever

-I am nothing without you

-The ghost of him

-My pink little star

-Generational curse

-Pain of letting go

The beauty of love & self-love

My sweet baby, my sweet boy.
Please don't text me to tell me you love me.

My sweet baby, my sweet boy.

I want to hear it from your lips,
not from the chime of that ringtone,
the ringtone that chimes just for your nickname.

My sweet baby, my sweet boy.

The kind of chime that will send goosebumps chilling down the back of my spine.
But if you insist on writing it out for me, love.

My sweet baby, my sweet boy.

I want you to write it out with your lips,
covering mine in sugar,
forever and infinity.

My sweet baby, my sweet boy.

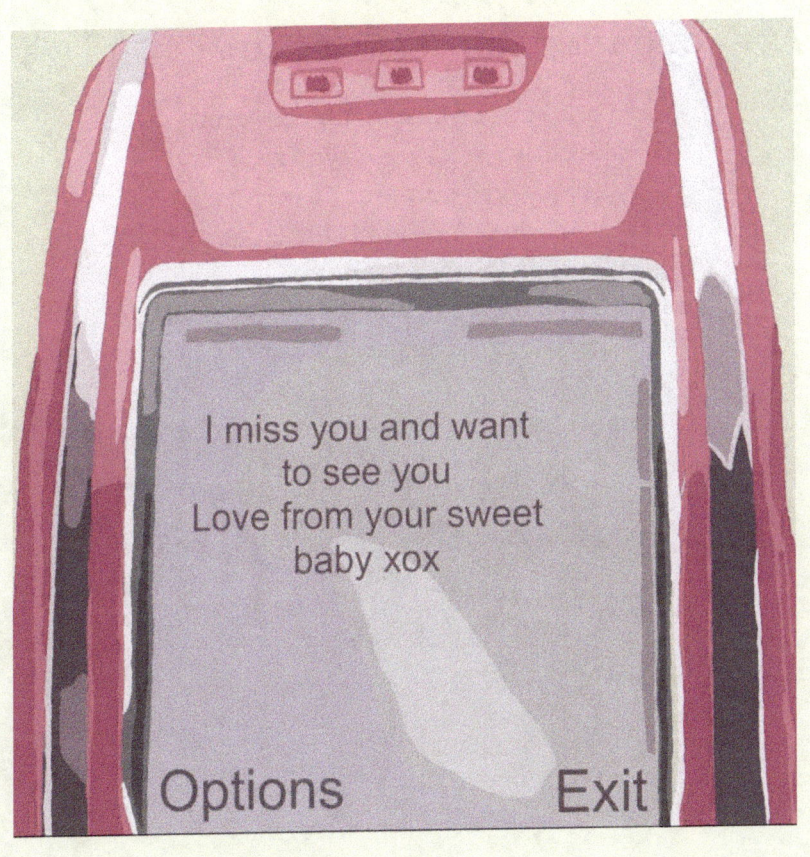

Art created on the rose

Rose in between my thighs,
where you placed your lips,
keep eye contact with me,
while I sweeten you with every kiss.
You eat it so well,
effortlessly, that my senses ignite,
I get so close to blooming that my thorns may prick,
the art you create, so bewitching that it makes me twitch,
lapping every layer.
It makes my rose blossom every time.

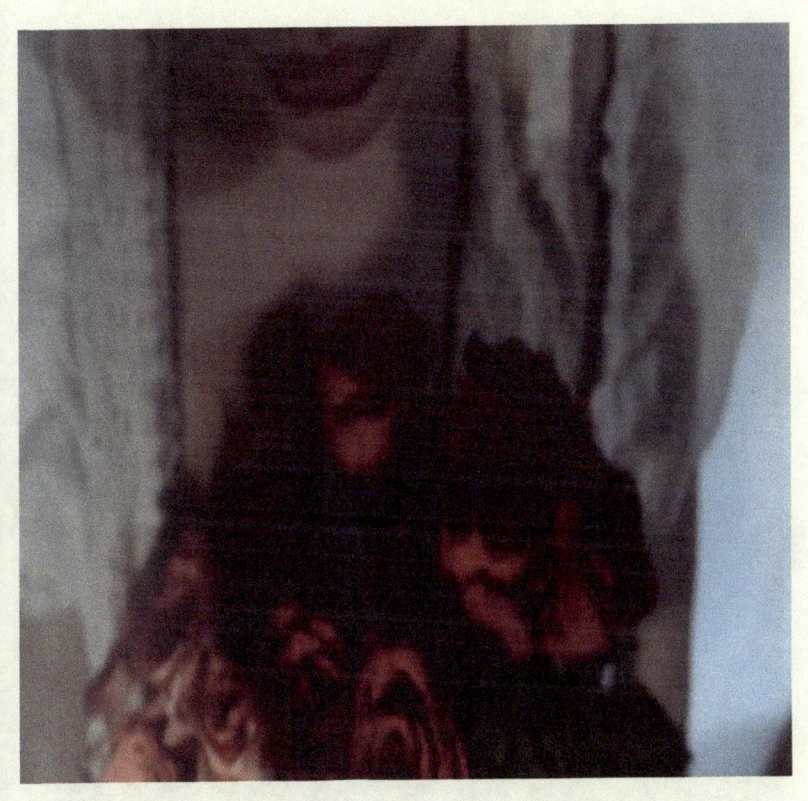

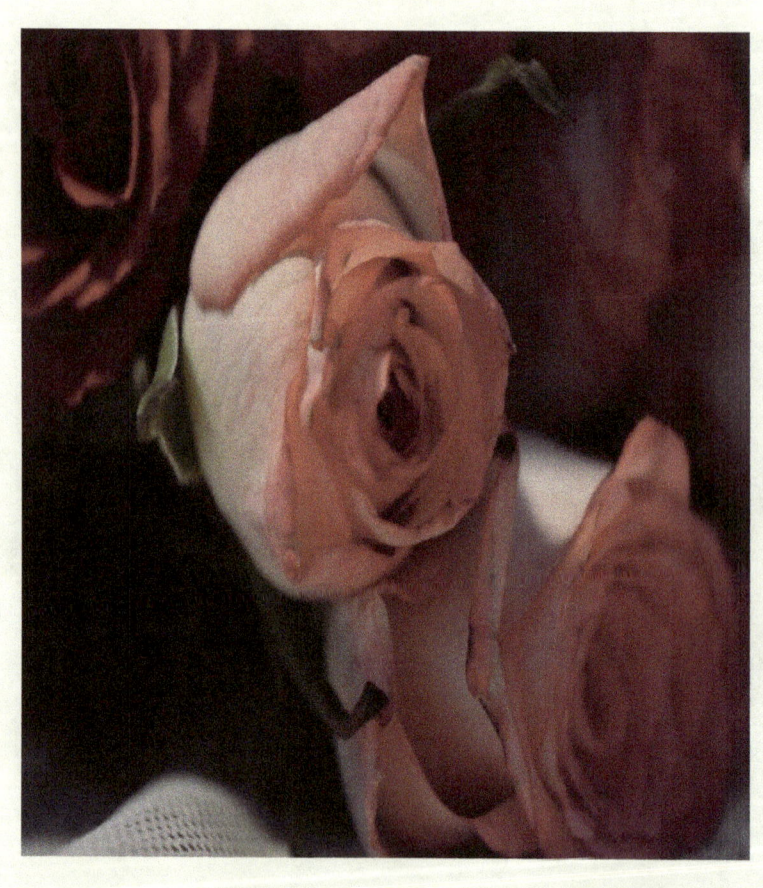

Sweet as sugar.

My sweet baby, my sweet boy.

He is so sweet,
so sweet his kiss left sugar all over my lips.
His sugar sweetens my bitterness.
Bitter black coffee, sweetened with his love,
his taste is so sweet,
too much of his taste will rot my teeth.

My sweet baby, my sweet boy.

Filled with so much sugar,
pouring his sweetness all over me.

The eyes.

> The gateway to the soul,
> the recognition of beauty,
> blue like the tide's ins and outs,
> the eyes that stare through my soul,
> the eyes that never lie,
> your eyes, my love.

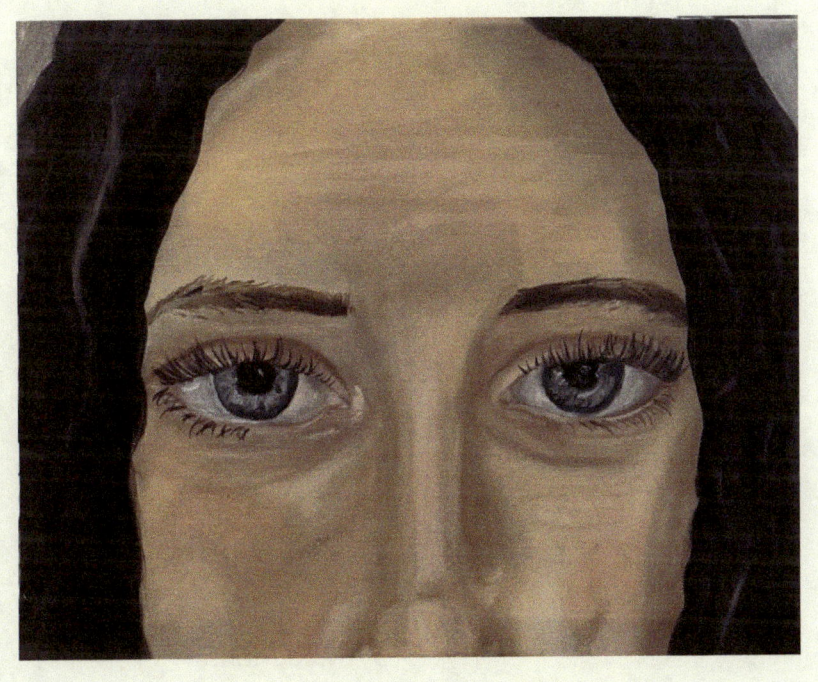

To
        experience
                          love,
                                    it

is

as

lucky

as

to

experience
                      happiness,
          it
                freshens

my

soul,

like
                           the
              fresh
                    summer

breeze,

blowing

through

my

face

on

the

fields

                                                                          in
                                          the

        countryside,

                                              where
                                                    I

experienced my first love...

Whispers in the night.

In the dim lit room,
shadows play.
Our secrets linger,
in the nighttime when everybody is away.
Our hearts alone in a sensuous dance,
we laugh and hold each other close,
not wanting to be apart.

My voice is like silk,
in a seductive display.
Me and my love kiss in the nights soft away.
Let me discover every inch of where your
secrets lay,
and every secret,
I'll lock and throw the key away,
never whispering them to another soul.
In the moon's tender glow,
shining love down our way,
hot and sweaty,
close together,
we'll dance till the break of day.

Fairies

A medium down south from me
expressed how the spirits showed her fairies
when she saw me,
flying freely around,
childlike personality,
creating magic and beauty.
I replied,
my mind is like a fairytale.
Romanticising every little detail in my life,
because otherwise,
how can I cope with the harsh reality that
happens inside my mind.
Fairyland is the real beauty,
the real beauty that keeps me sane, wild and
alive.

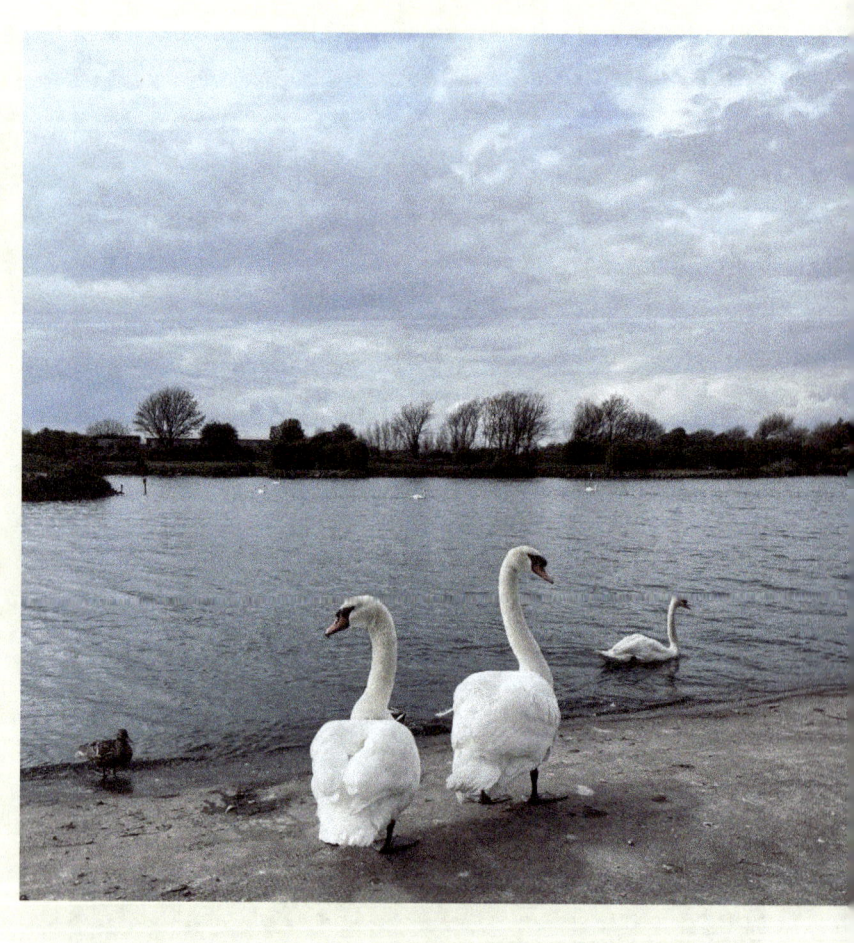

Empress or the other woman?

Maybe I was born to be the other woman,
looking for lustfulness,
gleaming in the shadows of the night,
his lips pressed against mine,
with words spoken that filled my empty soul
half full.
But when I look to the sky,
escaping those torturing daydreams,
I'm reminded of the beauty and power within me.
The love I hold in my heart,
the power from the rose that sits between my
thighs.
That I wasn't born for men,
or born to be the other woman,
but I was born an empress.
A soul so unique,
that if a man tries to destroy it
I suggest you pray for his mercy and soul,
because I am divinely feminine.
An empress born.

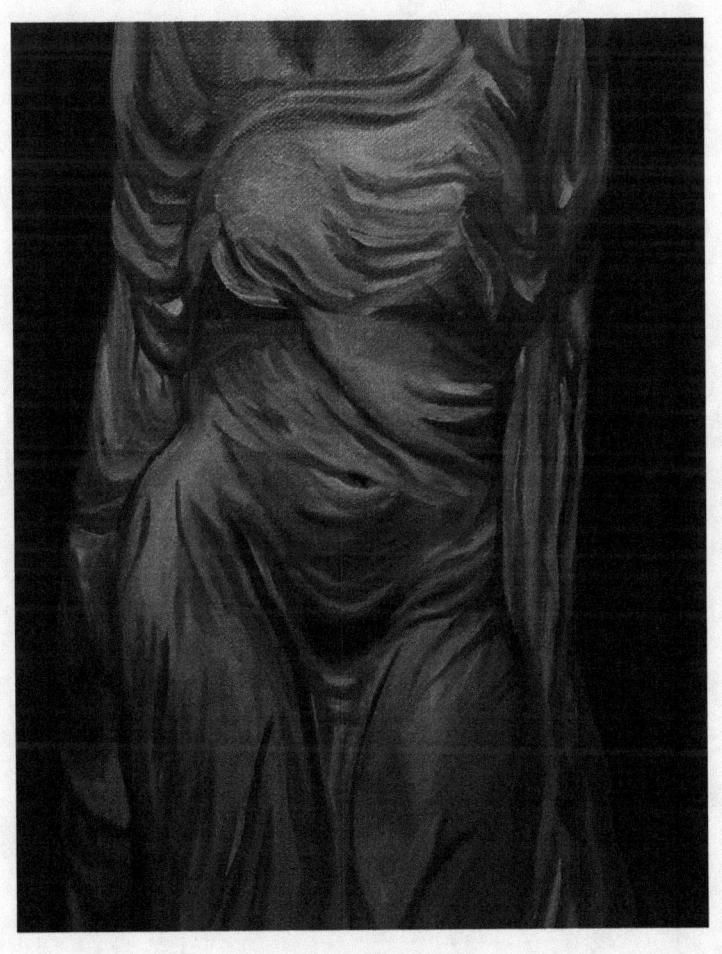

I am enough.

I am enough.

I am enough.

I am enough.

I am enough.

I am enough.

I am enough.

I am enough.

I am enough.

I am enough.

I am enough.

I am enough.

I am enough.

I am enough.

I am enough.

I am enough.

I am enough.

Definition

What those men did to you, doesn't define you.
You are a woman,
you are strong and powerful.
That's what defines you.

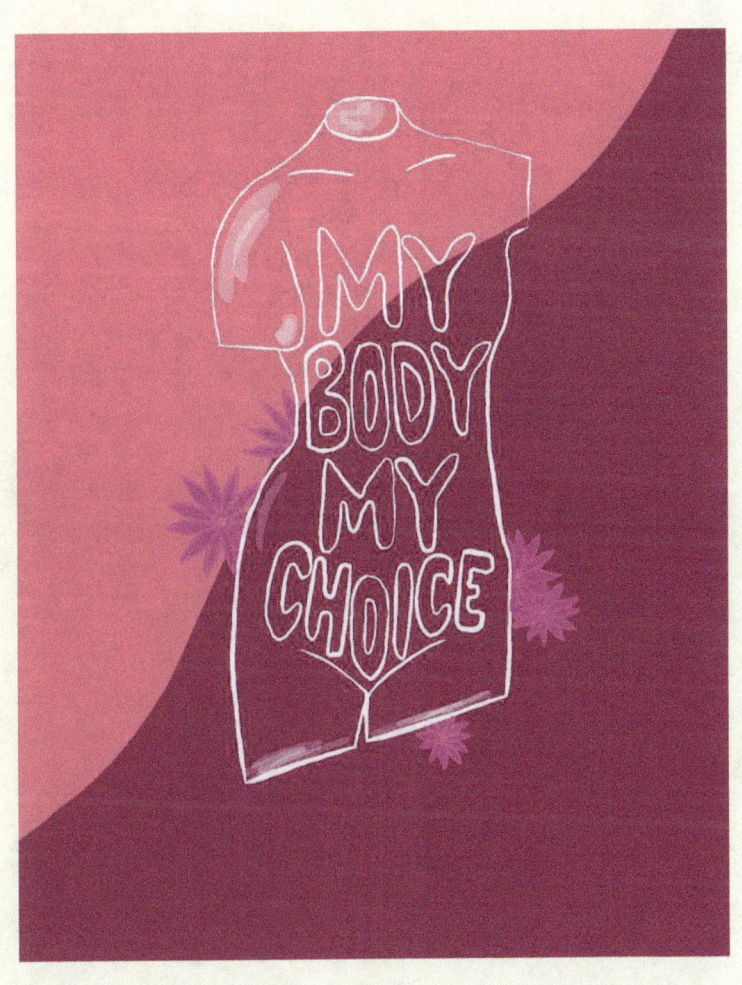

Sea

        The tides ins and outs,
        her gracious beauty,
        doing what she loves,
          unapologetically.
Brushes through the shells and the sand,
   the roaring crashes onto shore,
the waves flow with her graceful energy.
The land where Aphrodite was born.

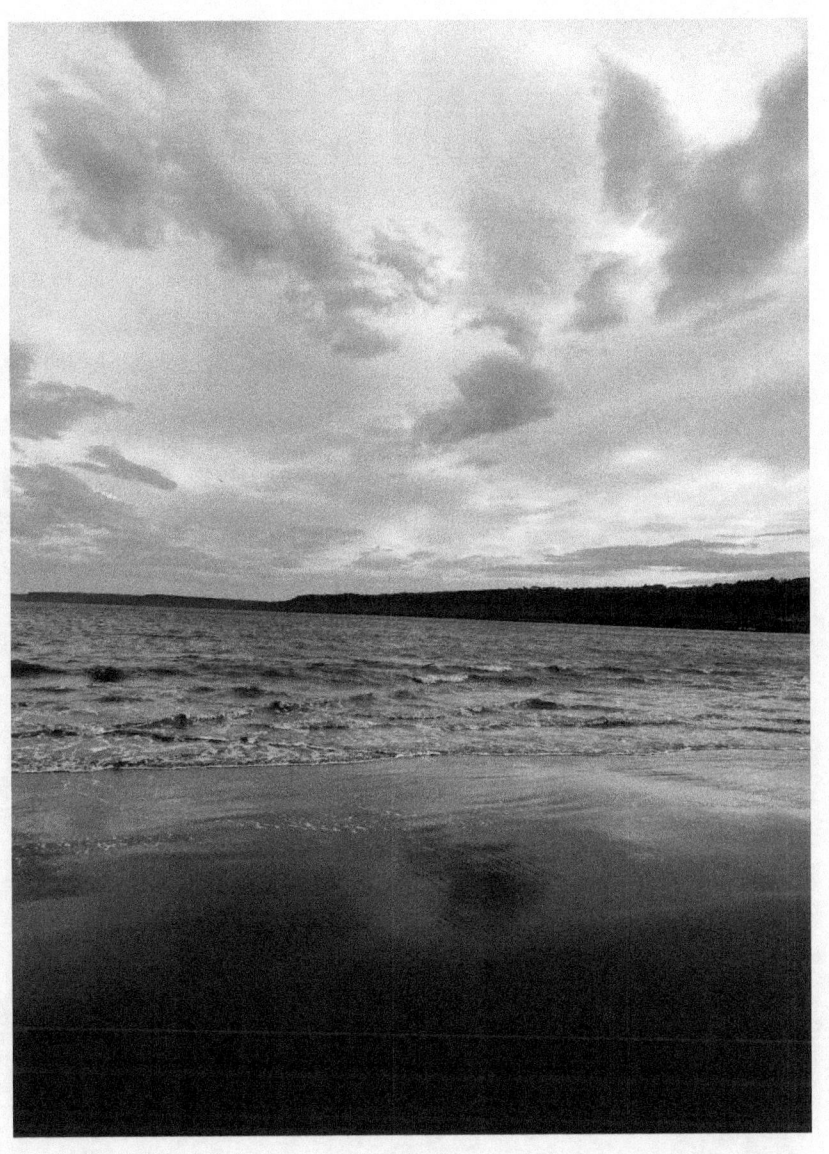

As I spread my wings,

angelic I shine

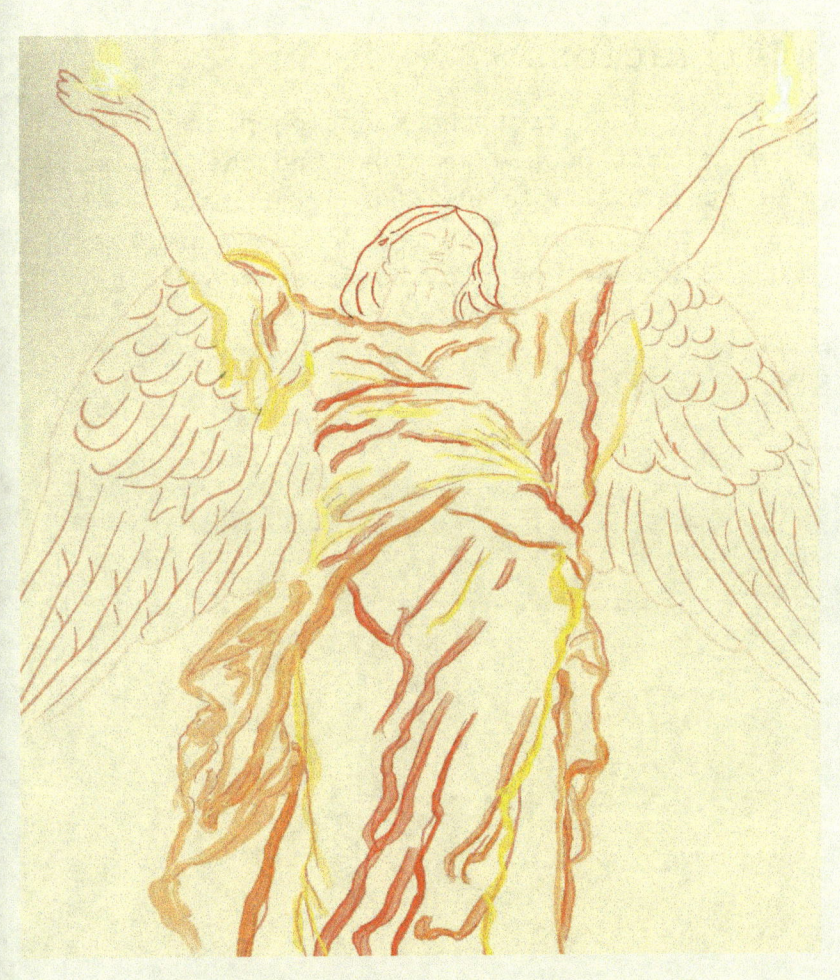

Affirmations

I attract the right people,
I attract people who love and cherish me,
I attract people who can communicate well,
I attract people who respect my boundaries,
I attract people who treat me well,
I attract people who inspire me.

1111

Not his show girl.

He wanted me to be his show girl.

Bare and naked,

blowing and puffing on my cigarette,

at night with him by my side.

A glass of red to wash those nerves to shore.

But by day,

alone, as he went away.

I couldn't comprehend with that pain.

I'd buy myself roses.

A rose to lay the situation to rest,

but also, to remind me of my feminine nature.

A beast at her best

and when that beastliness came to life,

her beauty would blossom,

and when man tries to cause carnage to that blossom,

she'd come fourth with rage,

not doubt.

Roaring thunder,

screams and crashes,

her feminine energy is courageous,
because she knows her worth.
By day and night,
she does not play a showgirl,
but simply puts herself first.

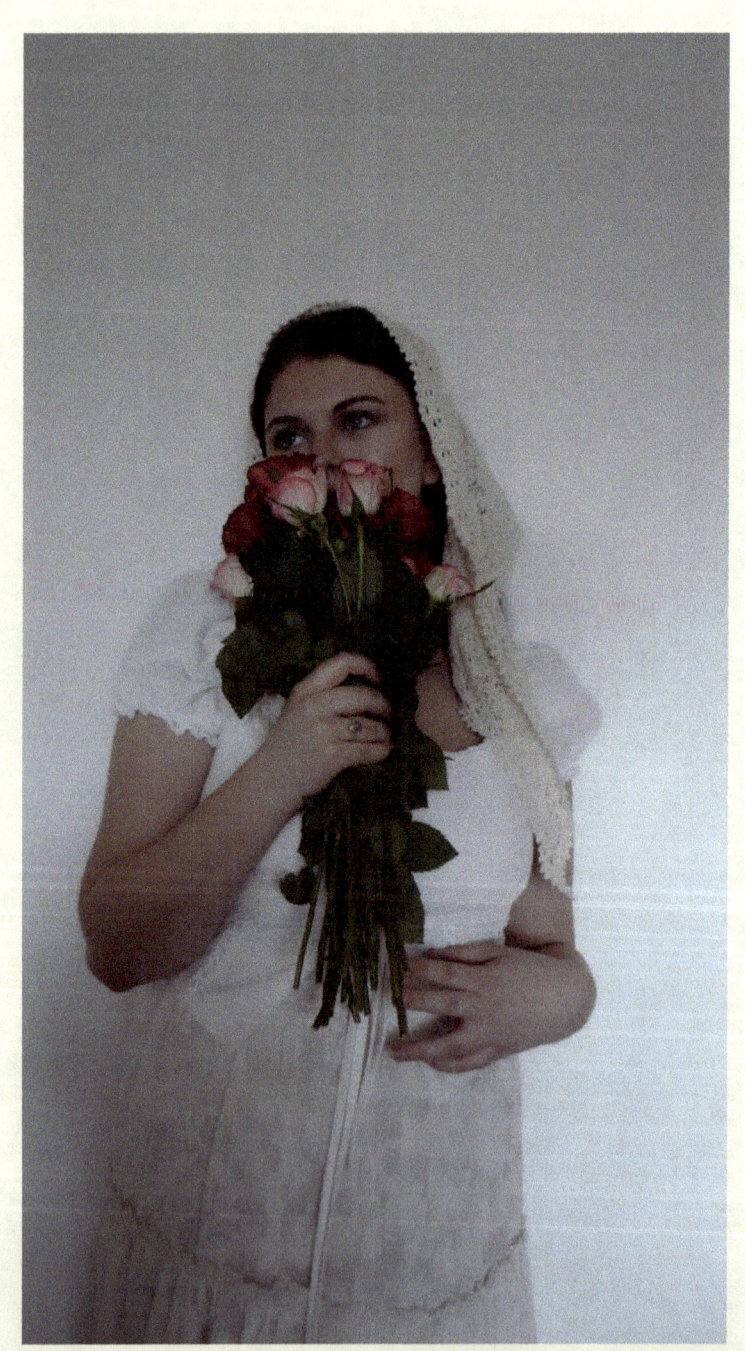

The poisonous venom from love.

Scribble

Scribble

Out my heart

Your dream girl?

     Am I that girl you dream of?
Or is it easier just to have me around?

The memory of him from before has gone,
I don't even know who he is anymore.

I want to be free,
but something always holds me back.

Caught up in this dance,
of a cruel romance.

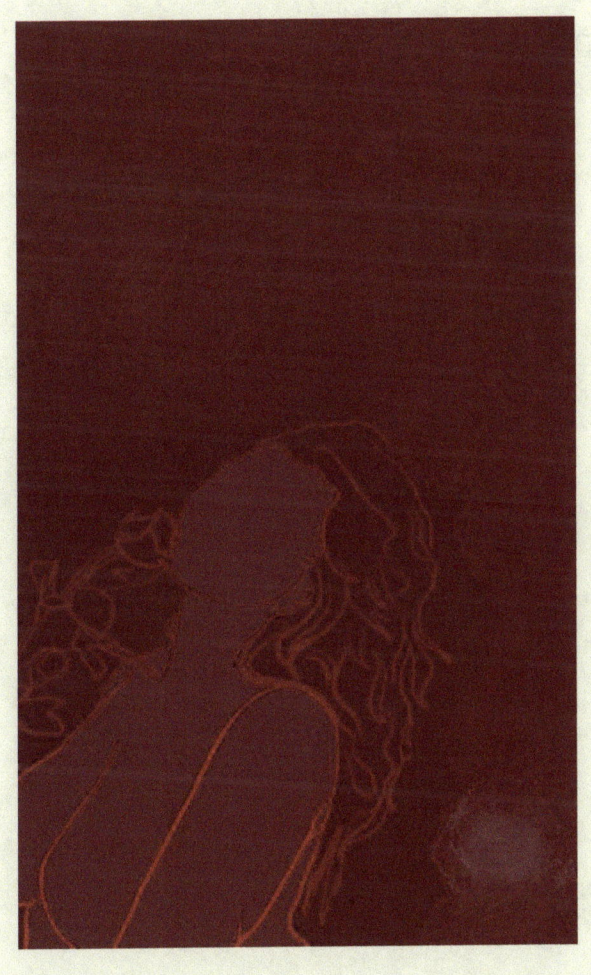

An angel's ego

May the love burn through the sorrow of my soul,
mind bombardier, with the voice of an angel,
with his abusive words,
an ego too good for his own.
My, my, the angel sores me with his beauty,
violates my heart and soul.

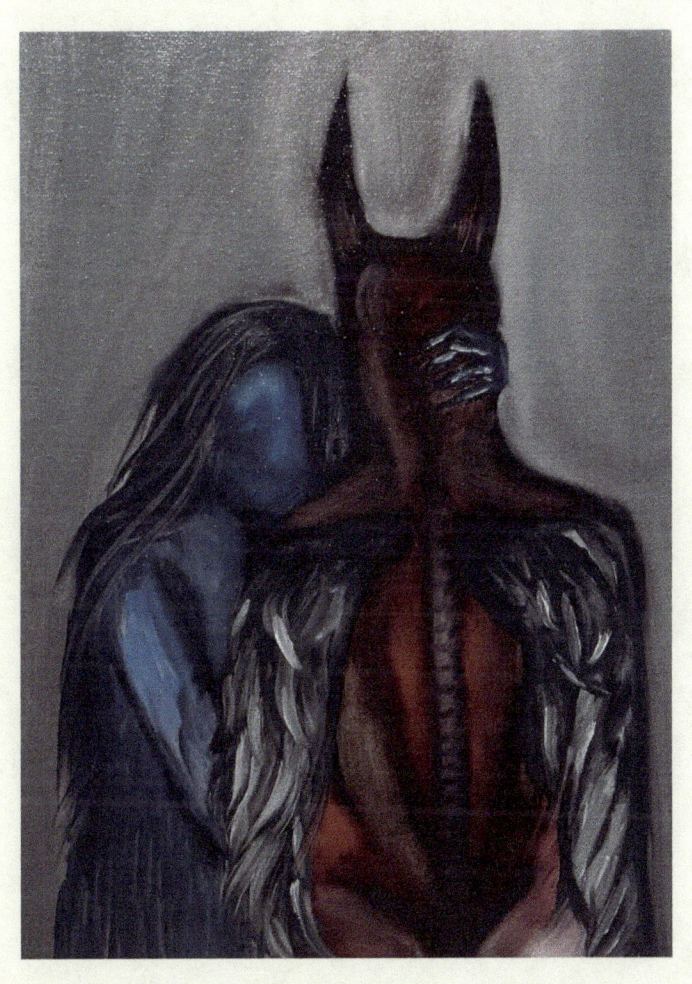

Snooker bar.

In that smoky room,
love's allure does sway.
A riddle in the shadows,
but it finds its way.
With cannabis smoked words,
he blows, I puff,
just like this we create heartache art.
Love's mystery grips,
tearing us miles apart,
all night I lament for him,
a haunting refrain.
But in this snooker bar,
we reunite again.
In love's tangled web,
we play in vain,
seeking more solace,
but lost we may be,
in the enigma of this love's tragedy melody.

Show girl.

I'm his little show girl,
blowing and puffing on my cigarette.
I'll pose for you honey,
just keep me sweet.
Tell me you love me, to keep me on my feet.
Degrade and hurt me,
I'll still be your little girl.
A loveless love,
but with him, adrenaline is on top of this world.

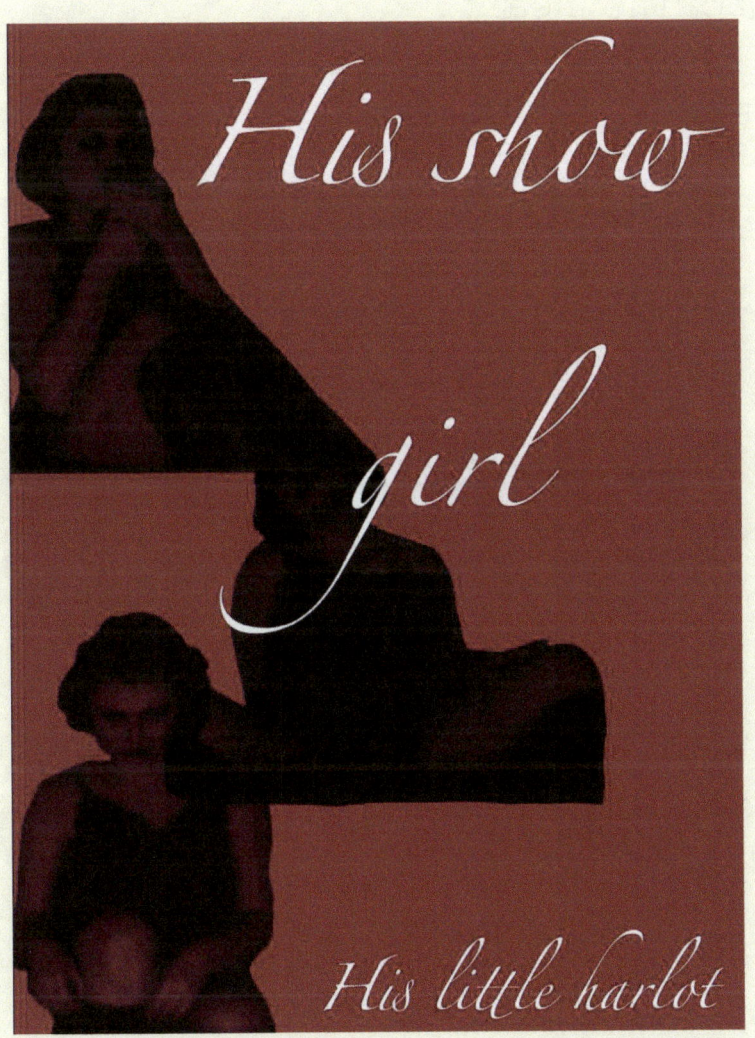

Cocaine heart.

His tongue smothered in toxicity,
spoken words that shattered my heart to pieces,
unable to fully ever be repaired.
His a bad man,
but I love that man,
I love every beat of his cocaine heart.

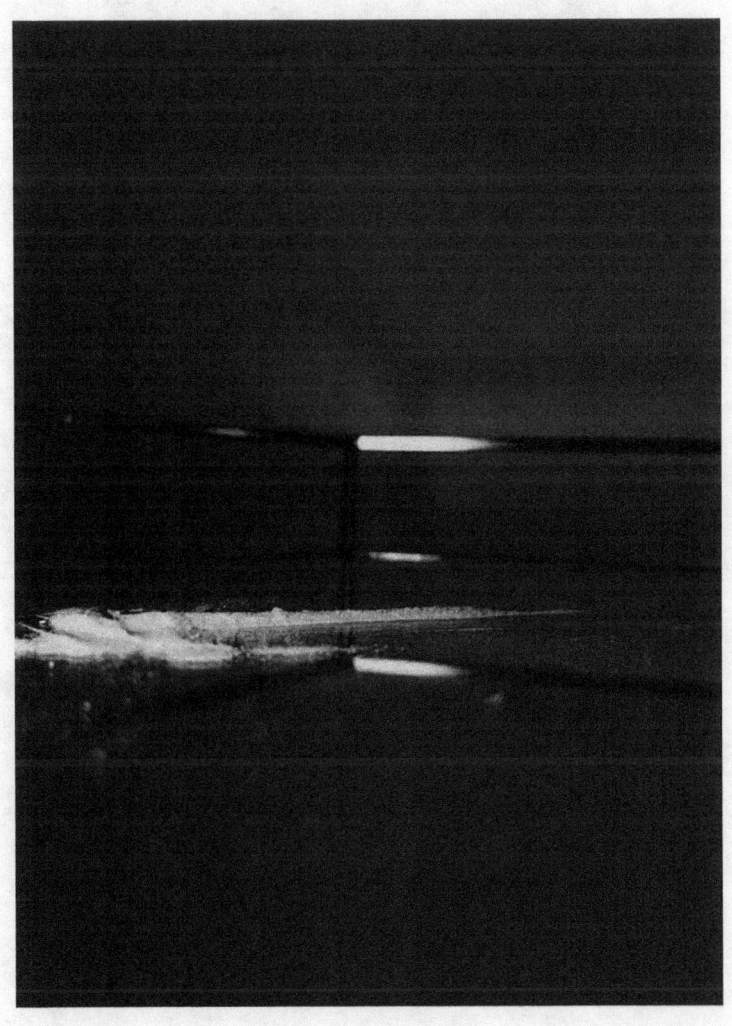

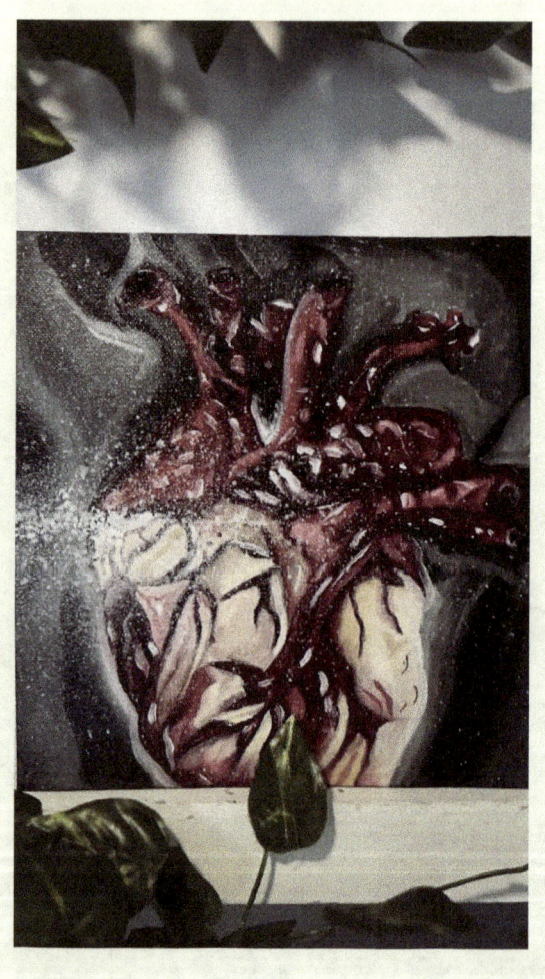

Craving for love, not lust.

Just a girl,
craving for love but left with lust.
I want to feel numb on the tips of my lips,
where I've been smothered and stained from drops of alcohol,
filling my blood with poison and with every bit of that poison I start to feel sane again,
I feel okay,
like I filled my sorrows and sadness into a glass and downed it for them to drown away.
Burning a flame onto mother nature tobacco leaf,
which was intruded by man,
to create poison that will crisp the organ that gracefully breathes in air,
creating a tumour which man wants to cure,
and all for what?
A few minutes of dizziness.
To feel my blood run round my body in seconds to make me numb.
Breathing in the smoke and then releasing all the stress.

Breathe in.
Breathe out.
Breathe in.

Breathe out.

Love is the medicine I crave,
but this is how I stay sane.
My body became a map filled with fingerprints, tracing up and down my body in appreciation and lust. His fingers flying up and down me like the devil among the rosebuds, but lust was all it ever was. I'd lie next to them with nothing but emptiness, regret and loneliness.

I'm not the real love that was on their mind. Not their first heartbreak, not the first eyes they gazed into,

but just another girl.

Every weekend the same routine.

Just a girl, empty and alone.

Thinking about a heavenly, wholesome love.

Craving for love but left with lust.

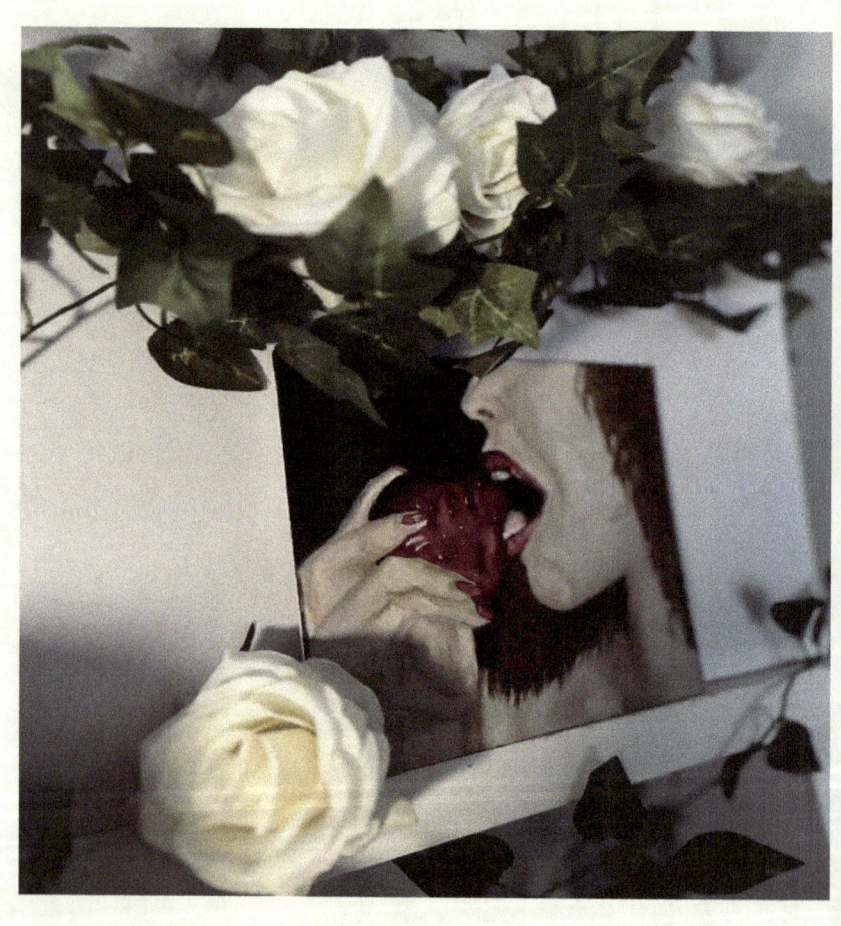

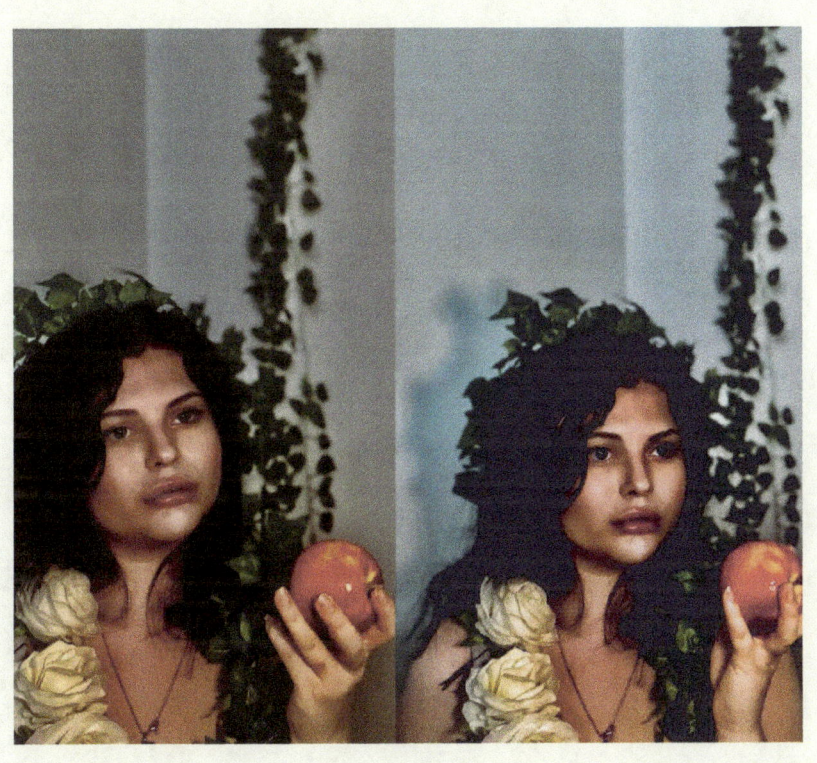

Falling away.

You're falling away!
Silence is louder than I imagined,
untouched, unspoken.
Your body's here, but your mind wanders.
I would do anything for you and I,
my love.

Loneliness

Loneliness lingers in my home,
he puts your foul moods in order.
He grabs me by the throat, so I can't breathe.
He makes me wonder where all my friends went.
My loneliness tells me you're lying if you tell
yourself you're ok.

HD & Replay

Do I entertain you like your other women?
Dressed down tired and blue,
isn't she in HD replay?
Doing what you like,
while I'm "arrogant" in my slumber.
I'm just tired and blue.

Do I entertain you like your other women?
While I do your chores,
she plays in HD.
Don't forget my love,
I'm just tired and blue.

Do they listen to your melancholy cries?
But I have to scream for you to hear me.
Do they conquer your desires seductively?
But I need tutorials and trials to meet your expectations.
Do they sound sweeter than I?
While the crow crooks from my throat as my senses are enlightened.

Why do you replay your other women?
When you leave me on replay with the feeling of being forgotten, tired and blue.

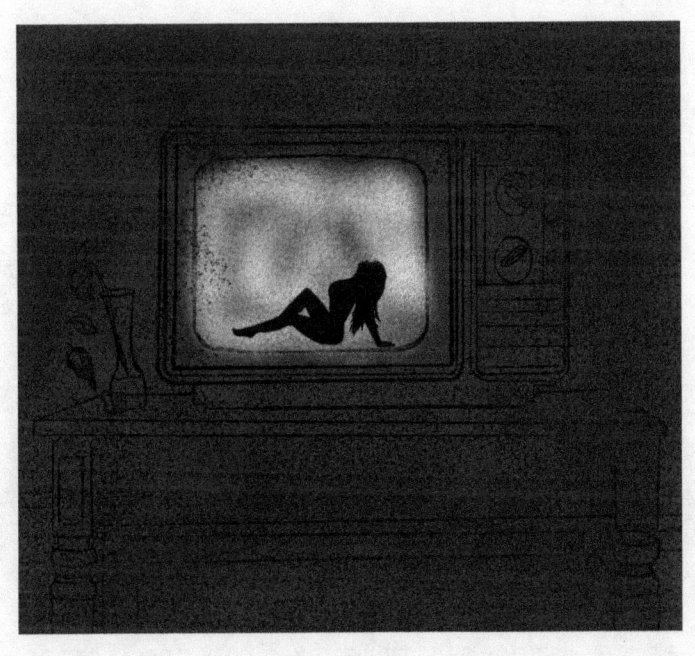

Caution Flammable

You tell me I'm the chaos,
the one creating the fire,
while you stand there with the petroleum and matches.
Third degree burns covering every inch of my angelic soul,
hell is all over me.
While your distractions let me burn,
they add more fuel to the flames,
that spit!
That screech!
Blinded by the sparks.
I don't want to turn to ashes,
while you stand there and watch me burn.
Let me rise as a phoenix from the flames,
ash to an angel.
Your fuel will run out soon,
And I will be burnt out to ashes,
Those ashes will blow away.
Disappear,
forever gone.

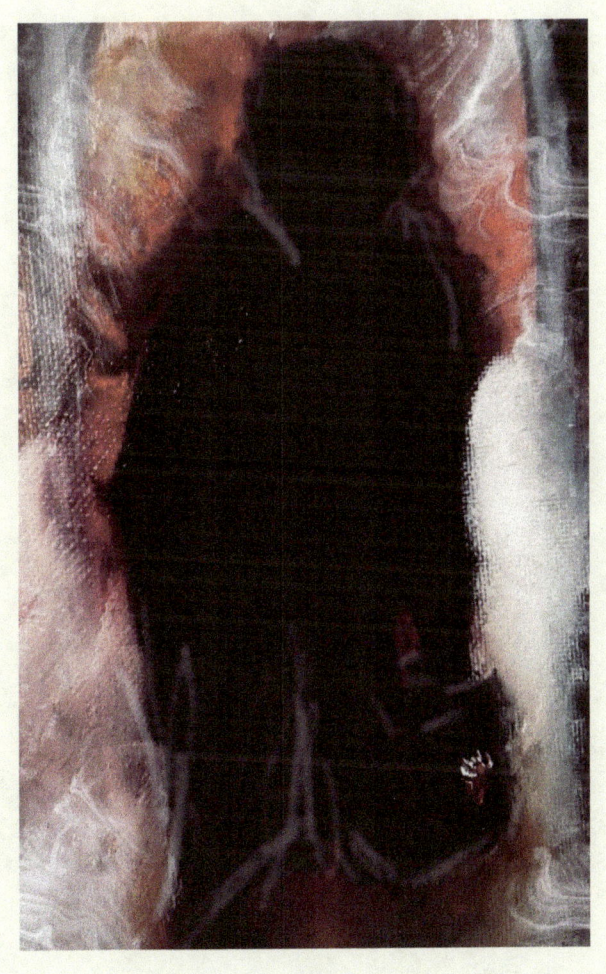

Fragile masculinity

        Blank canvas,
with the shape of destruction through it.
     I'll frame it,
   title it, fragile masculinity.

Be free, be free, be free

I sat alone,
I waited quietly for you,
but you abandoned me in your bitterness.
I carry everything on my shoulders.
Be free, be free, be free,
I constantly repeated,
be free, be free, be free,
as I swallowed the lump in my throat.

He says he understands me, but still leaves me
alone and blue.
Makes me feel like he doesn't know me at all,
not even a clue.

I don't want this sorrowful life,
struggling through this hot and cold.
I want to be free and wild.
Be free, be free, be free.
Away from you and your melancholy

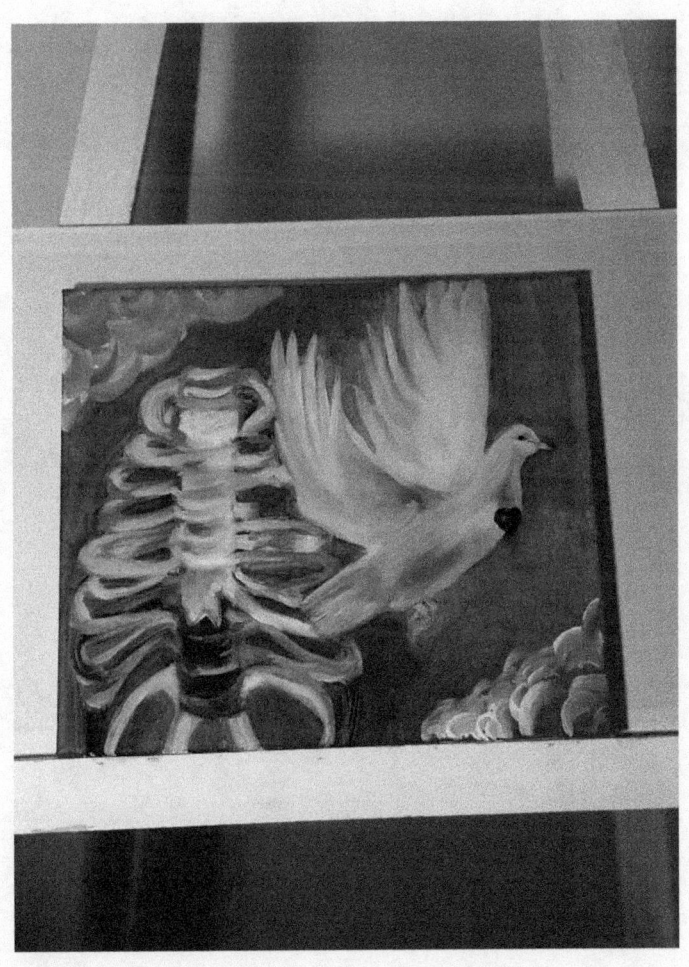

A cruel dance of violence

A cruel dance of violence,
dark and bleak,
in the shadows,
where innocence is meek.
The steps of anger,
a brutal choreography,
on every beat,
two hearts entwined in a tragic allegory.
Set me free and let me live out to the end of this show.
Cold and naked,
covered in the markings of your touch.
Bow to the crowd and end this at once.

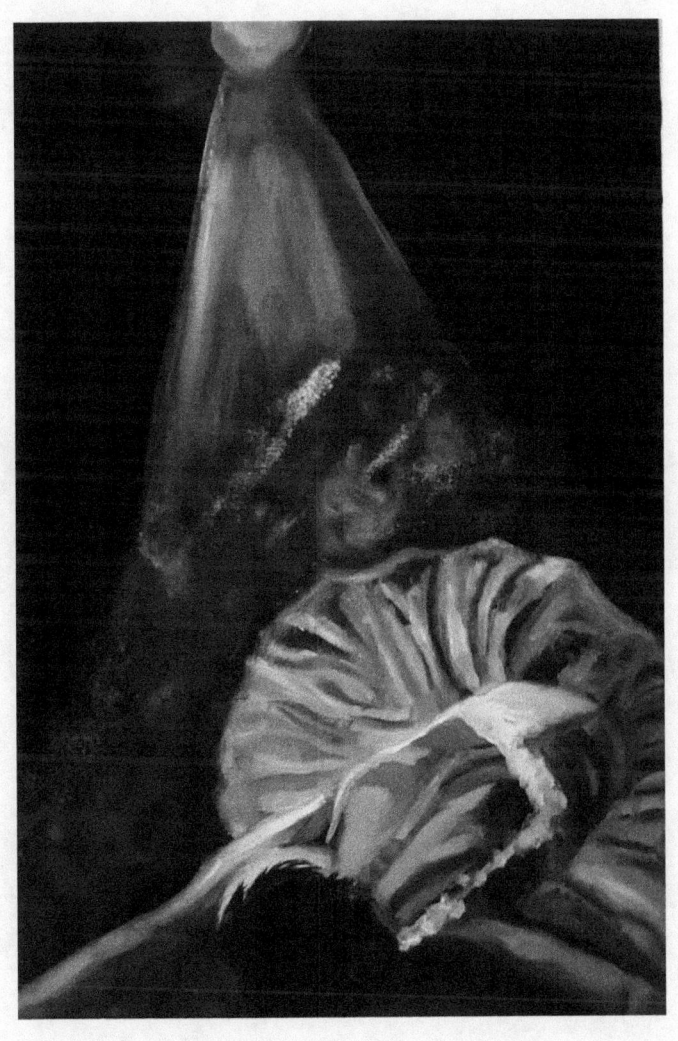

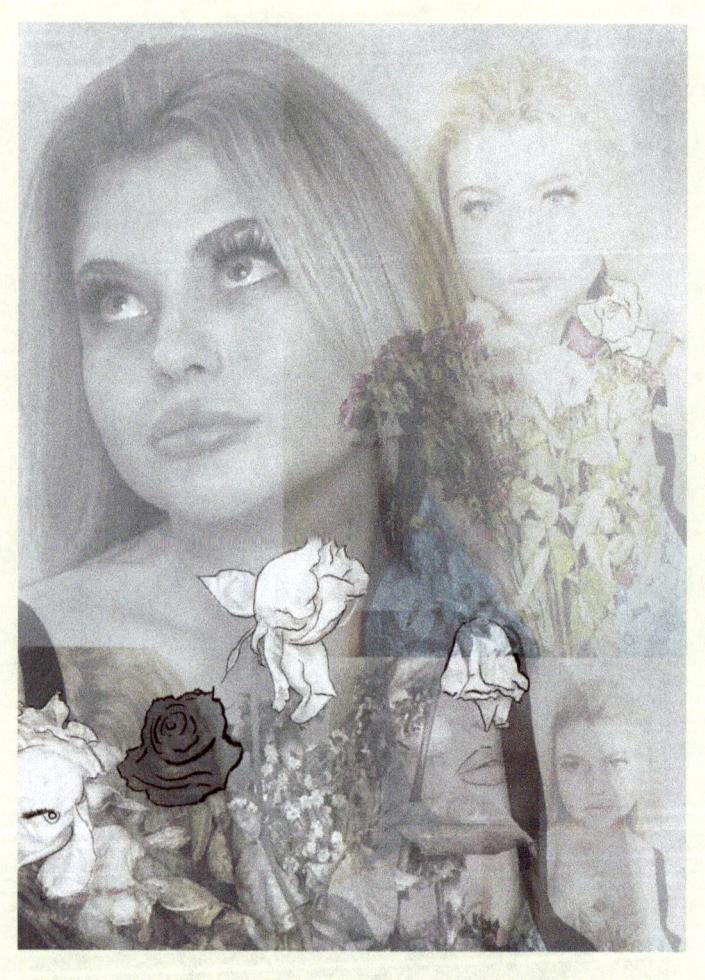

I wished for our forever

I looked at him and dreamt for our forever chapter,
he held me and dreamt of this moment.
Forever was never in his cards

I'm
    N
     O
      T
       H
        I
       N
        G
                Without you

The ghost of him.

As I lay next to him,

he is here,

haunting.

But not mine to hold,

not mine to love,

nothing but cold.

Here next to me,

lays the ghost of him,

and I am forever alone.

My pink little star

When you went to that foreign land,
with no choice but to depart,
I gave you my pink little star,
a piece of me to keep you safe.
But you still couldn't make sense of me and my pink little star,
took her pink little shine and hid her in the dark.
Watching you from afar,
with her dim light,
my poor, poor, pink little stars shine.

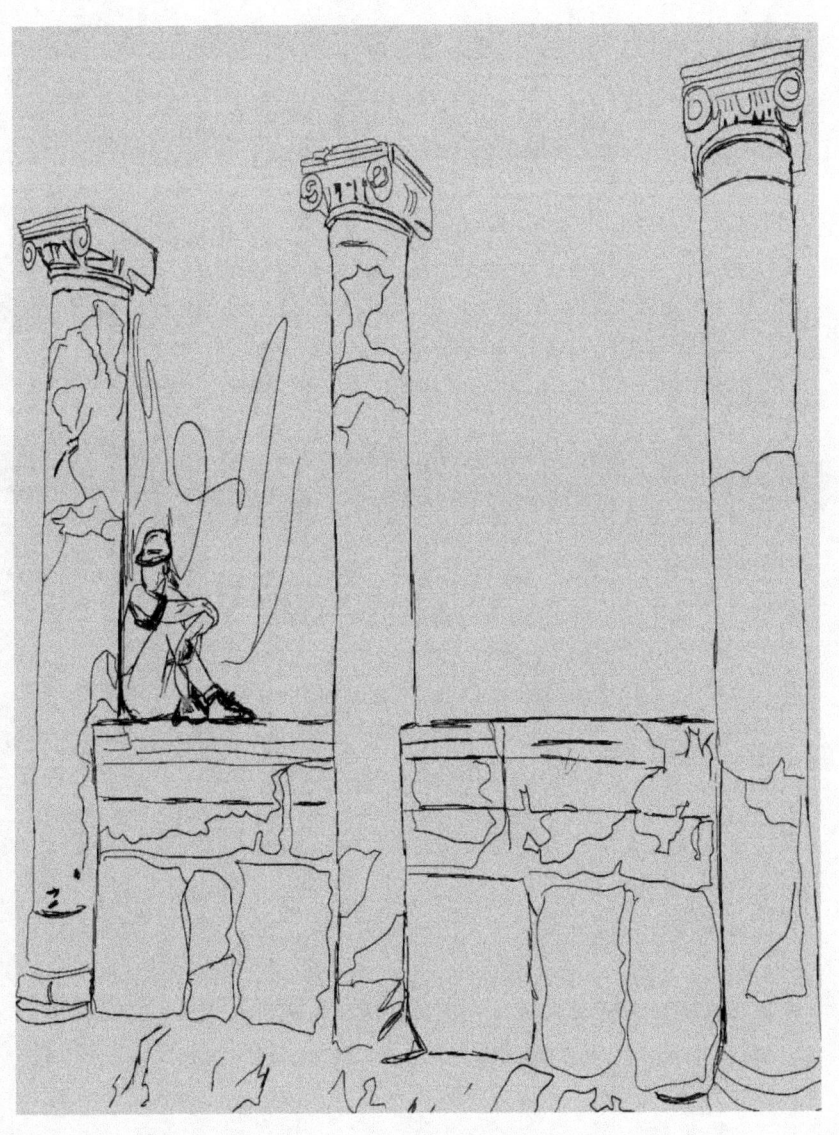

Generational curse

Lines of history abuse,
fathers to mothers,
fist to face,
that's the curse of my family.
Why was I born a woman?
Scared of this curse running through my veins.
Desperately wanting to be loved.
Tired of my thoughts being beaten, broken and blue.
Blade deep through my skin.
Please,
oh please!
Let me break this curse,
this sinister generational curse,
so, my daughter is free,
my grandchild raised safely,
and I,
I will finally be at peace.

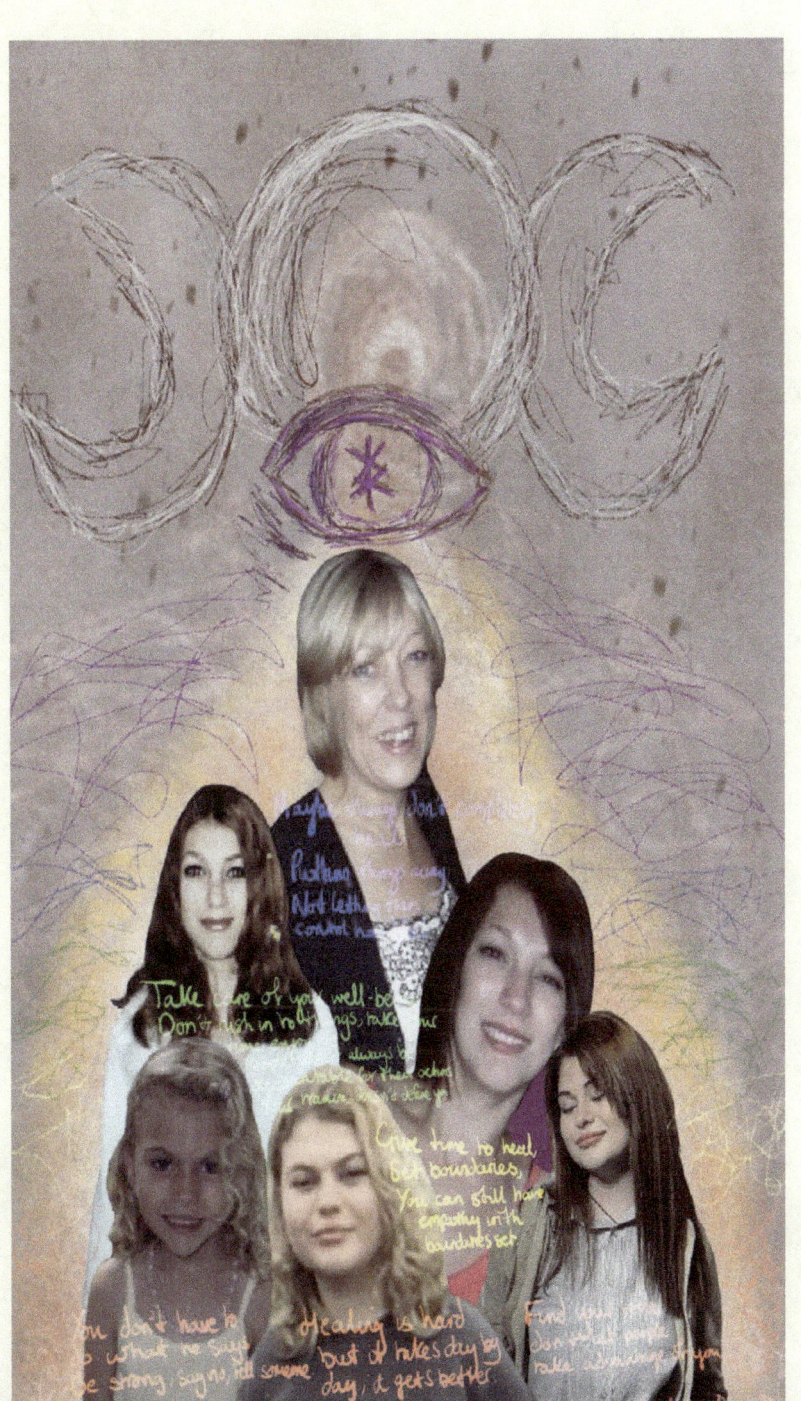

Pain of letting go...

It's so hard for me to let go,
but my wounds are so deep,
my soul is bleeding out from my wrists,
leaving me feeling weak,
with no strength left,
nothing more to do,
nothing but
to let go of you.

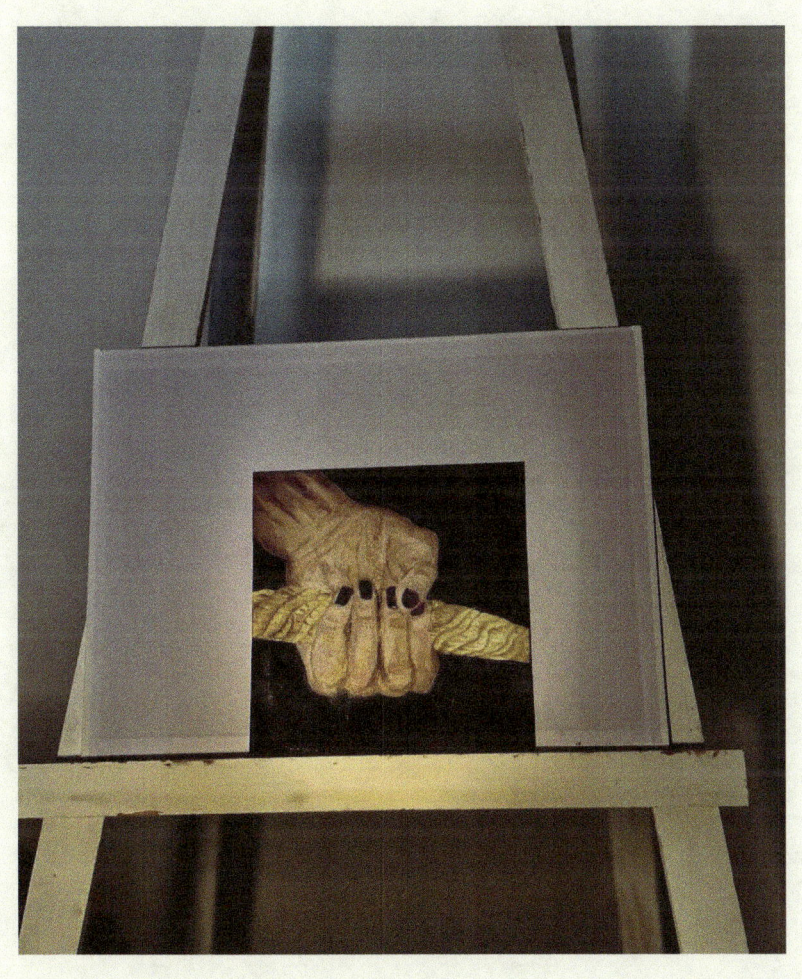

If you are a victim of domestic violence whether that is mentally or physically, please call these numbers or in an emergency contact the police.

United Kingdom contacts.

National Domestic Abuse Helpline UK: 24/7 service- 0808 2000 247

Womens Aid- 0845 345 4345

Men's advice line- 0808 8010327

Emergencies police line- 999

Non-emergencies police line- 101

The Mystery of Love
Daisy Mai Hilton 2024 ©

www.ingramcontent.com/pod-product-compliance
Lightning Source LLC
Chambersburg PA
CBHW050232230526
45470CB00005B/1910